Charlotte Mason

THE TEACHER WHO REVEALED WORLDS OF WONDER

I AM, I CAN, I OUGHT, I WILL.

BY LANAYA GORE

ILLUSTRATED BY TWILA FARMER

BLUE SKY DAISIES

CHARLOTTE MASON

THE TEACHER WHO REVEALED WORLDS OF WONDER

By Lanaya Gore
Illustrated by Twila Farmer

Published by Blue Sky Daisies
Wichita, Kansas
blueskydaisies.net

Library of Congress Control Number: 2022933259

ISBN: 978-1-944435-26-4

AUTHOR'S NOTE

At the time of Charlotte Maria Shaw Mason's life, England was in the midst of figuring out how to educate all the children of its nation. Girls were now going to school along with boys. Schoolrooms were set up for poor and middle-class children. Laws were passed that protected children like Oliver Twist from working long hours in factories and workhouses.

The bright minds of the time were searching for an approach that could educate all. Trained teachers were needed. Mothers and governesses wanted guidance on preparing their children for a good life and a love of books and learning.

Miss Charlotte Mason was there to help children learn to read, write, and think. She loved schoolrooms full of boys like Tom Sawyer and girls like Anne Shirley who could be shown how to see with bright eyes and a keen mind—her "bairns" she called them. Miss Charlotte hated to see bored, nervous, distracted children waiting for school to be over. She knew that "education is a life."

Her method has become popular because she knew how children naturally learned. She emphasized learning for all of life, not just for the purpose of attaining high grades, glowing praise, or a high-paying job later. She loved children and wanted them to love learning. This story tells about Miss Charlotte Mason and how she found and practiced the distinctives that make up the Charlotte Mason method.

Pat-a-cake, pat-a-cake! Baker's man!

The little girl giggled with glee when her mother got to the end:

> *Mark it with a "P"!*
> *and put it in the oven*
> *for Popsey and me!*

The mother smiled and returned to her book as Charlotte took out her "doll houses," which were pretty snail shells.

Born in Bangor, Wales, on January 1, 1842, Charlotte came from a line of Irish Quakers who were schoolteachers and textbook writers. Her siblings were much older than Charlotte, and she grew up with few playmates—a quiet, thoughtful, self-composed girl.

Her earliest memories were of the sea. She loved the sea!

She was playing with her father in the sea one day, and he slipped and dropped little Charlotte in the water. Her mother had been swimming some distance away, and she swam with vigor toward Charlotte. The situation was only a trifle. Charlotte was safe by the time her mother reached her. Still, her mother's alertness and quick movement struck Charlotte as a great benefit, and physical fitness would later be a part of her training in habits.

Books were precious in her home. Charlotte remembered "crouching by the fireside, clasping her knees and listening" as *Anne of Geierstein*, one of Sir Walter Scott's Waverly novels, was read aloud to her. The Waverly novels became favorites that she would read over and over as an adult. She remembered looking at the pictures in a dry, heavy archaeology book on Nineveh. Reflecting on this helped her realize that even young children are interested in a range of knowledge that might surprise adults, and it is worthwhile to offer it to them.

Charlotte received the famous book by Daniel Defoe, *Robinson Crusoe*, as a gift for her eighth birthday. And she would grow up to give books as gifts to the special children in her life, with personal inscriptions for each of them. Later in her life, she would say, "Never be without a really good book on hand."

Teaching seems to have been a natural calling for Charlotte. Some of her Quaker family had been teachers.

One day she watched a tall lady with a dark shawl walk down a shady path near her home followed by a train of children holding onto her skirts. Charlotte spent some time observing this graceful lady and her classroom. She greatly admired her and knew "that teaching was the thing to do, and above all, the teaching of poor children like those I had been watching."

Charlotte would indeed get the chance to teach very soon, for she began a student teacher apprenticeship at age 12!

This would have been hard work for a young girl. She would assist a head teacher with 40 or so students, collect their weekly pence from the parents, inquire about absences, and clean up the school after students left. In the winter, this left her going home alone in the dark—a scary venture for her! *"Thou art my hiding-place; Thou shalt preserve me from trouble; Thou shalt compass me about with songs of deliverance."* These words would "beat in her brain, over, and over, and over the whole length of the way, evening by evening, winter after winter."

That Bible passage from Psalms would surely also have been a comfort to her when her mother died from illness when Charlotte was 16 years old. Her father followed in death just five months later, leaving Charlotte alone in the world. Her family had been poor, so they had not left her any money to live upon. Her father had seen to it that she be accepted into her student-teacher apprenticeship, but it paid very little.

Charlotte must have been sad and lonely, but she did not give way to despair. She left in December of her seventeenth year for London. She would take the examinations to try for the Queen's Scholarship, which would allow her to attend college.

To win the Queen's Scholarship, Charlotte had to take nine tests, each of them lasting three hours. She would answer questions such as this one:

> "Write out from British History any narrative which you think would interest children aged eight to ten years on one of the following points: a) courageous perseverance under difficulties; b) readiness to suffer on the side believed to be right; c) uncertainty of fortune."

The tests covered history, Bible, geography, arithmetic, grammar, home economics, drawing, music, and classroom management. Whew! The students were exhausted when the exams were over!

Charlotte passed with a rank of 141 out of 275 students. She and her friend did not pass drawing. But she had made it! She earned the Queen's Scholarship, which would pay for the two-year teacher training.

During her time at college, a pattern surfaced in Charlotte's life that would continue for some years—a pattern of working too hard, becoming ill, and having to take a break from the work. She did not have family to visit over the holidays. She always had close friends throughout her life, but one can imagine how strong a young girl must be to carry burdens and make decisions without parents to rely upon. The stress began to have long-term effects on her health. "Heart trouble" would be the diagnosis later in life.

Charlotte started out doing well in the training school. But when it came time for her critique, when she would have to teach a lesson while a training officer observed and criticized her, Charlotte showed signs of distress. She was anxious and her nerves got the better of her. Mr. Dunning, one of the observers, wrote to her afterward to try to comfort her:

> *My Dear Miss Mason,*
>
> *I was very sorry indeed this morning when I found that giving a lesson was too much for you. When I saw you first I was exceedingly pleased thinking you were better and strong and not nervous in [being observed]. Indeed, I felt as if you had lost all fear of me as a critic and regarded me as a friendly genius sitting there to do you a good turn…You must not attempt another [such lesson]…You can teach well and need only to study our principles. I liked your lesson much…I hope [your] affliction does not lead you to repine. You may be young in years but rich in experience and to <u>suffer</u> perfects more and faster than to <u>do</u>. Thus you are brought to be more like the Saviour…I could not leave comfortably without scribbling this note. I was so grieved [to watch you suffer].*
>
> *Affectionately,*
>
> *R. Dunning*

Because her first year did not end well (perhaps for health or stress reasons), the Home and Colonial Training Institution (affectionately called the Ho and Co) offered Charlotte a position at an infant school in Sussex. Infant schools had children as young as toddlers and up through seven years old.

Charlotte would not have to take the second year of college. She would later take the exams after a year of teaching and gain her teaching certificate in that way.

Charlotte's life as a young adult was filled with teaching, lecturing on education, and observing children. She loved the children in her school and the children of her friends. She wrote, "How I wish you could see my children—some are such sweet little cherubs, and some such noble little Washingtons, and some such tiresome little monkeys." She had the opportunity to observe the nieces and nephews of a close friend in their home. This was dear to her since she never married and had no children of her own.

One day, Charlotte noticed that her friend's five-year-old niece was saddened by seeing a homeless man while she was on a walk. Thinking about how concerned the girl felt for the man, Charlotte realized that a child is just as much a "person" as an adult. Children know right from wrong, are generous, sincere, imaginative, and have great capacity to learn. They lack the knowledge and experience that grown-ups have, but they are every bit as much *persons*.

While spending time with these bright children, Charlotte thought she could teach the seven- and eight-year-olds English grammar. Their aunt insisted that children could not understand grammar, but Charlotte wrote up lessons to give it a try. She discovered that it was too abstract; the children would have none of it! "I was allowed to give the lessons myself with what lucidity and freshness I could command; in vain; the nominative case baffled them…"

She was observing and discovering so much about children and the way of learning that was natural to them. Charlotte began to collect her ideas about teaching children into a set of principles. One principle she saw clearly was that each child is unique. One child will take to music and another will excel in reading; but all should have a chance to connect with many areas of study—a generous feast of learning!

Another principle she discovered was that children gained deep understanding and knowledge through *narration*. Narration is a word that means "telling what you know." Charlotte encouraged her students to tell what they knew after a lesson or a reading.

Charlotte noticed that short and varied lessons fit the physical and mental capacities of a child. She believed this was better for young children than long sessions at a desk.

She saw that the power of observation was a more natural way of learning than stuffing facts into one's head. Charlotte wanted *living* books and stories for her students, which brought an ease and joy of learning that a textbook or a teacher-focused lecture did not.

Charlotte also found that children made many connections across subjects. They might notice a poem mentioning Penelope and Odysseus, which brings to mind the wandering adventure in *The Odyssey*, which likewise might bring to their minds the wandering Israelites of the Bible.

By de-emphasizing grades, Charlotte's method of teaching decreased competition and increased eager, joy-filled, soul-learning.

All of these became part of Charlotte's principles for education.

Charlotte published her first book when she was nearly 40 years old. She had taken a journey—on foot and by train—exploring the English countryside. It had been a marvelous time, and Charlotte had written in a journal all that she had seen. These notes helped her to write *The Forty Shires*, a book about the history, scenery, arts and legends of England's shires. It was a success, and she was asked to write more.

She next worked on a set of geography books. Charlotte remembered a geography book from her childhood from which she'd had to memorize lists of rivers, towns and exports. She did not enjoy that part of the book, but she *did* enjoy the footnotes in which people who lived in the region would tell anecdotes, which were little stories about the places. She decided to write geographies for children with the flavor of story instead of lists of places to be memorized. Teachers and students would use that five-volume *Elementary Geography* set for many years to come.

Charlotte attended St. Mark's Church and wanted to contribute to their fundraiser for a building project. As a way to help, she offered to give a series of eight lectures on education. These were well-received and were soon collected into a book called *Home Education*, the first book of her popular six-volume series on the topic of education. This was a launching point for the rest of Charlotte's life's work. Parents wanted to use Charlotte's ideas with their children and began organizing meetings to discuss how to do that. The group would be called the Parents' National Education Union, or the PNEU. They published *The Parents' Review* magazine to provide guidance for implementing Charlotte's ideas in education, home life, and child training.

Charlotte moved to a lovely, small town called Ambleside and became known as Miss Mason. Ambleside is nestled in the Lake District of England, an area where a number of famous writers have lived, including the poet William Wordsworth and Beatrix Potter, the creator of Peter Rabbit. It was here that Charlotte opened a school to train girls who wished to become governesses or teachers, or who wanted to prepare to be good mothers and aunts. She called it the House of Education.

The opening year of the House of Education saw the arrival of four students. One of those students, Violet Parker, recollected,

"How well I remember that night of 15th January, 1892. A cold but lovely drive by coach from Windermere to Ambleside: trees heavily laden with snow on one hand—a black lake on the other, a mysterious and wonderful fairyland to our delighted eyes.

At the end of our journey—on arrival at Ambleside there was a warm welcome from Miss Mason who so soon won our hearts. Whatever our surroundings might have been, we should have been happy merely to be with her!"

21

As the House of Education began training students, Miss Mason was still immersed in her work for parents and children all over the British Empire. She was publishing *Parents' Review* magazine (which many people still read today!). She wrote the plans and book lists for mothers teaching their children; such schools were called Parents' Review Schools. Later, teachers from her House of Education would begin little schools using her method, and school administrators would use the principles in the public classrooms of England.

Charlotte also created "Mother's Education Courses," a mail correspondence course. Moms taking the course answered monthly questions on a reading assignment.

During these years Miss Mason wrote and published the rest of her six volumes on education. One of these, the book *Ourselves*, is written for students on the matter of character.

Miss Mason was dearly loved and respected at Ambleside. She had the generous support of friends and co-workers who helped her personally in times of illness and assisted her in the work of educating. But was it only a work of educating?

One grateful future teacher remembered her first day at Ambleside. Miss Mason asked her why she was there. Puzzled, she answered, "I have come to learn to teach."

Then Miss Mason said,

"My dear, you have come here to learn to live."

To Miss Mason, education was *life*. It was not a grade—not a set of facts to be learned or a list of books to be read after which one could announce pridefully, "I am done! I have completed the list and am therefore educated!" No, this was not true education! Miss Mason believed that "the getting of knowledge, and the getting of *delight* in knowledge are the ends [or goals] of a child's education." Miss Mason was convinced that a successful education sparked a desire to continue learning even after finishing school.

Miss Mason said, "Education is an atmosphere, a discipline, a life." She created an atmosphere of wonder and delight at the House of Education in Ambleside. She established discipline through a routine for herself and for the girls who were there for training. The routine made time for everything to get done without worry, without rush, and without overemphasis spent on any one thing.

Miss Mason began her day answering letters and dealing with the details of running a household, for she ran the House of Education very much like a home. Then would come the writing of articles or book reviews or grading narrative exams. She would take a morning break by reading *Punch*, a humorous magazine, for a few minutes and then turn back to her work with renewed energy. Ten minutes before the midday meal, she would read a bit of a classical author. Charlotte purposely included both heavy and light reading in her routine. She had dinner with the students and often had a poem or a joke to share. She enjoyed a bit of humor and loved listening to her students' jokes and riddles.

The course of her day continued with interspersing work and reading, spending time with company, and taking some rest. She gave attention to the task at hand and did not worry over unfinished bits when it was time to move on to another task.

Oh, and nature! How important time in nature was to Miss Mason. She took daily walks (these became carriage drives when she could no longer walk far) out in the country air. She chose Ambleside for teacher training, in part because of its beautiful natural setting. The students also took afternoon walks to enjoy the fresh air and exercise, observe nature and geography, and keep their own nature notebooks. Miss Mason would share her nature finds with the students at mealtime and ask them to share their own. She might describe a flower, ask them if they knew what it was, and leave them to figure it out if they did not.

God's creation throughout the Lake District provided a life of education in so many ways. It was a place of relaxation, exercise, natural history (the study of plants and animals by observation), geography (lakes, waterfalls, hills), geology (fossil finds!), and beauty.

The girls at Ambleside remembered that Miss Mason brought out the best of one's self. She had high expectations, but they found they could rise to the occasion despite doubt in themselves. She knew that persons—children and adults alike—had great and diverse potentialities and that given the right tools and atmosphere they could fully blossom.

She might quote a bit of a poem at mealtime and ask her students to memorize it and share it with the group in the evening drawing room.

Sometimes she'd ask the girls to put on a play or come up with some kind of evening entertainment when company happened by.

Miss Mason herself was interested in a great many subjects and ideas. She would invite visitors to Ambleside to teach a skill such as basket weaving or paper folding or to give a lesson on an artist. Various people wrote articles for *The Parents' Review* magazine and it was often on subjects that interested them—not necessarily directly related to education.

She wanted to inspire teacher and child alike with great and varied ideas. This is why students today who learn according to Charlotte Mason's methods may have a great number of subjects to cover over the course of their school life. Miss Mason wanted to open a wide room—she called it offering a generous feast—so that persons would come to know God and many people, places, and things. After learning something for the first time, encountering it again would be like recognizing a familiar face. The generous feast would be food for the mind and the soul far into the future. Miss Mason was continually learning herself and encouraged her students to never stop learning after graduating from the House of Education at Ambleside. She warned them to "not for a moment suppose that you can warm yourselves and others for months together upon the original stock you brought from Ambleside. Every day new 'thoughts that burn' must be supplied or the fire will go out and present the dreariest of all spectacles, a desolate hearth."

One question a teacher must answer is, "Who is the teacher?" You might say, "The teacher is the teacher, of course!" But Miss Mason said a teacher should be careful not to get in the child's way. As one little girl said, "Mother, I think I could understand if you did not explain quite so much."

A person can learn by reading a living book or looking at a map or studying an artist's print and having an idea—a living idea—strike him. A thought from an original mind can go straight to the mind of the child. The mother or teacher can answer questions, ask a thoughtful question, or point out a simple observation; she is not necessarily silent. But the children will do the work of education themselves. They will attentively meet with worthy ideas, and the teacher or parent, who is also a learner under authority, will help guide them with wisdom.

When Charlotte Mason traveled to Florence, Italy, she gazed in wonder upon a fresco on the wall of a Spanish chapel. Miss Mason saw that the fresco answered the question, "Who is the teacher?" She called it "The Great Recognition." The fresco shows the Holy Spirit descending upon the minds of men, both religious and secular.

"The great recognition, that God the Holy Spirit is Himself personally the Imparter of knowledge, the Instructor of youth, the Inspirer of genius, is a conception so far lost to us that we should think it distinctly irreverent to conceive of the divine teaching as co-operating with ours in a child's arithmetic lesson. But the Florentine mind of the Middle Ages believed that every fruitful idea, every original conception whether in Euclid or grammar or music, was a direct inspiration of the Holy Spirit."

Who is the teacher?
God is the teacher.

All true knowledge, whatever the subject, belongs to the Creator God and is given by Him to the pupil. Miss Mason had a reproduction of the fresco hung in the House of Education at Ambleside, so students would also contemplate this idea of God as their teacher, even in such "non-religious" subjects as grammar and algebra.

Charlotte Maria Shaw Mason was a dark-haired, blue-eyed sober little girl who gave her life in the service of educating all—poor and rich, girl and boy alike.

She offered a method of schooling that has crossed cultures and generations and given so many families, schools, and homeschools a natural way to train and educate.

She worked until the last days of her life and passed peacefully in her sleep at 81 years of age.

Charlotte wrote to school children:

It is a delightful thing about this School of yours that the Scholars love their books. When all the papers reach me I often say, "this is a very happy week for me." I am happy because your papers show me that you have had a delightful term's work and that you LOVE KNOWLEDGE.

I think that is a joyful thing to be said about anybody, that he loves knowledge; there are so many interesting and delightful things to be known and the person who loves knowledge cannot very well be dull; indoors and out of doors there are a thousand interesting things to know and to know better.

There is a saying of King Alfred's that I like to apply to our School. "I have found a door," he says. That is just what I hope your School is to you—a door opening into a great palace of art and knowledge in which there are many chambers all opening into gardens or field paths, forest or hills. One chamber, entered through a beautiful Gothic archway, is labeled Bible Knowledge, and there the Scholar finds goodness as well as knowledge, as indeed he does in many others of the fair chambers. You see that doorway with much curious lettering? History is within, and that is, I think, an especially delightful chamber. But it would take too long to investigate all these pleasant places and indeed you could label a good many of the doorways from the headings of your term's programme.

But you will remember that the School is only a "Door" to let you in to the goodly House of Knowledge, but I hope you will go in and out and live there all your lives—in one pleasant chamber and another; for the really rich people are they who have the entry to this goodly House, and who never let King Alfred's "Door" rust on its hinges, no, not all through their lives, even when they are very old people.

I have a great hope for all you dear Scholars. Other people will be a little the better because you love knowledge, and have learnt to think fair, just thoughts about things, and to seek first the Kingdom of Heaven in which is all that is beautiful, good and happy-making.

I am,

Your always affectionate friend,

C. M. Mason

LOOK BACK AND FIND

THE HUMBLE RUSH PLANT

The "humble rush" was chosen as a symbol for the House of Education students' <u>L'Umile Pianta</u> magazine and for their badge. They weren't sure if they should choose the lark or the "humble rush," but a lady spoke up to say that the rush should be chosen, for it could bend to every wind, never breaking, however bent. It would remind students to listen for and to consider every trend of educational thought while holding fast to their own principles.

THE SKYLARK AND THE DAISY

I AM.
I CAN.
I OUGHT.
I WILL.

The children of the Parents' Review Schools (later called Parents' Union Schools) were asked to send in ideas for a badge for themselves. The final badge design was a circle of daisies with a skylark in the middle and the motto "I am. I can. I ought. I will." written under the bird. The daisy was a symbol of childhood, and the singing skylark was to remind the children of joyful energy. The daisies were later removed to make a simpler design.

"THE GREAT RECOGNITION" PAINTING

The fresco is actually titled "The Triumph of St. Thomas Aquinas." It shows (not pictured here) the Holy Spirit in the form of a dove descending on several groups: first the Madonna and the Disciples, then upon the peoples who heard the gospel preached in their own language at Pentecost. Next there are three dogs who represent animals who share in the gentleness poured out by the Holy Spirit. Seven virtues come next (Faith, Hope, Love, Temperance, Prudence, Justice, and Fortitude). Then come (pictured here) a line of prophets and apostles, and under these are fourteen pairs representing the spiritual and natural sciences.

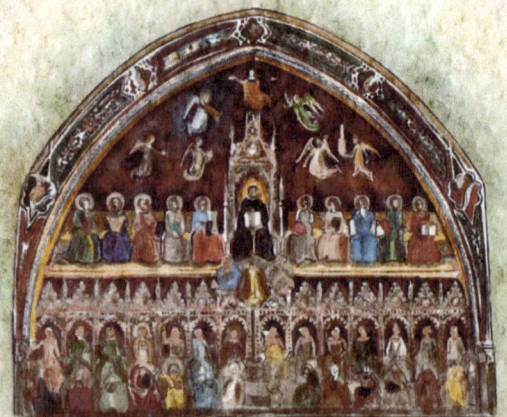

A GIRL SCOUTING FROM A TREE

The Boy and Girl Scouts owe their beginnings in part to a governess who had been trained at Charlotte Mason's college. The governess was teaching her young charge how to do scouting maneuvers from a tree. He "got" his father who passed underneath: "Father, you are shot; I am in ambush and you have passed under me without seeing me. Remember you should always look upwards as well as around you." From that incident, the father, who was General Baden-Powell, formed the idea of scout training for boys and girls.

THE WORLD OF WONDER IN NATURE

The natural world is full of wonder! Look for the Aurora Borealis (Northern Lights), peach Peonies, a Geranium house plant, a horse, a cat, and soft snow.

A ROOM FULL OF "BAIRNS"

"Bairn" means "child; son or daughter." It originates from Scotland. It is pronounced like the word "bear" with an "n" tacked on: "bearn."

A COACH AND DRIVER WITH A TOP HAT

Mr. Barrow was gardener and coachman at the House of Education in Ambleside for 30 years. He was Miss Mason's driver when she became unable to take nature walks. When asked by her friends why she did not have a motor car, she said, "I can talk to a horse but not to a motor."

MISS MASON AT THE DINNER TABLE

She enjoyed a good joke or riddle! One question she had for the lunch group one day was "What is the most precious thing to have in a house?" Some answered, "A bookcase!" or "A cradle!" Her eyes twinkled, and she said, "I think I would put space first."

A NATURE NOTEBOOK

Charlotte loved using notebooks as a tool. She suggested them for nature study, history ("Book of Centuries"), math, and commonplacing. Another name for a commonplace book is "Book of Mottoes" — for keeping favorite poems, songs, and quotes from your reading, or for other observations and tidbits of interest to you.

ABOUT THE AUTHOR

Lanaya Gore has written *Laying Down the Rails for Children* as well as other books that help homeschool families easily implement the Charlotte Mason method. She loves hot herbal teas, cozy books, hiking in the woods, and blogging about her family. Lanaya and her husband live in rural Missouri and are in the midst of homeschooling their four children.

ABOUT THE ILLUSTRATOR

Twila Farmer has been illustrating books and publications for over twenty years. For half of that time, she traveled internationally illustrating on location for nonprofit organizations. Twila now lives in Missouri. When she's not drawing, Twila homeschools her son, gardens with her husband, practices karate, and tries to keep their four cats from sneaking into the house. Twila will complete an MFA in Illustration through the University of Hartford in 2022.

SOURCES

Cholmondeley, Essex. *The Story of Charlotte Mason: (1842-1923).* London: J.M. Dent & sons, 1960.

Coombs, Margaret A. *Charlotte Mason: Hidden Heritage and Educational Influence.* Cambridge: Lutterworth Press, 2015.

Cooper, Elaine (General Editor). *When Children Love to Learn.* Wheaton, Illinois: Crossway, 2004.

Macaulay, Susan Schaeffer. *For the Children's Sake: Foundations of Education for Home and School.* Wheaton, Illinois: Crossway, 2009.

In Memoriam: Charlotte M. Mason. London: Parents' National Education Union, 1923.

www.ingramcontent.com/pod-product-compliance
Lightning Source LLC
Chambersburg PA
CBHW042007080426
42733CB00003B/33